Children's Publishing

Published by Ideal School Supply
An imprint of McGraw-Hill Children's Publishing
Copyright © 2002 McGraw-Hill Children's Publishing

All Rights Reserved • Printed in China

ISBN 1-56451-388-2

Send all inquiries to:
McGraw-Hill Children's Publishing
3195 Wilson Drive NW
Grand Rapids, Michigan 49544

Flip-Flash™ Spanish, Level II

3 4 5 6 7 8 9 WKT 07 06 05 04 03 02

The **McGraw·Hill** Companies

Helpful Hints for Learning Spanish

Flip and Check   Read the word on one side and say it in Spanish. Flip the page to see the word in English. Say the word.

Check the Difference
An article, such as *el* or *la* precedes Spanish nouns.
Some Spanish words include an accent mark.
Rules for capitalization and punctuation in Spanish differ from the rules used in English.

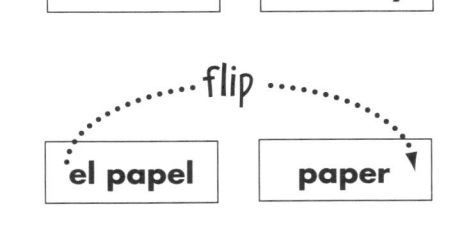

Use These Steps to Learn the Language!

Use these four steps to learn most words.

See it–look carefully at the letters in the word.

Say it–sound the word out.

Write it–write the word on a separate piece of paper.

Say it again–look at the word and say it again.

78 common English classroom terms and Spanish equivalents are included in *Flip-Flash Spanish™: Level II*. These words include:

- the days of the week
- common greetings
- commands used in the classroom
- names used for classroom supplies

- numbers
- times and
- simple sentences

lunes

Monday

martes

Tuesday

miércoles

Wednesday

jueves

Thursday

viernes

Friday

sábado

Saturday

domingo

Sunday

hola

hello

sí

yes

por favor

please

gracias

thank you

adiós

good-bye

siéntense

sit down

levántense

stand up

párense

stop

corten

cut

cierren

close

peguen

paste

pinten

paint

canten

sing

abran

open

dibujen

draw

contar

to count

escribir

to write

leer

to read

comer

to eat

hablar

to speak

beber

to drink

limpiar

to clean

dormir

to sleep

mirar

to look at

tocar

to touch

dar

to give

la escuela

school

el maestro

teacher (male)

la maestra

teacher (female)

la clase

classroom

el lápiz

pencil

el papel

paper

el escritorio

desk

el borrador

eraser

el cuaderno

notebook

el libro

book

la pluma

pen

veinte

twenty

veintiuno

twenty-one

veintidos

twenty-two

veintitres

twenty-three

veinticuatro

twenty-four

veinticinco

twenty-five

Vamos a contar.

Let's count.

¿Qué hora es?

What time is it?

las doce

twelve o'clock

la una

one o'clock

las dos

two o'clock

las tres

three o'clock

las cuatro

four o'clock

las cinco

five o'clock

las seis

six o'clock

las siete

seven o'clock

las ocho

eight o'clock

las nueve

nine o'clock

las diez

ten o'clock

las once

eleven o'clock

hora

hour

minuto

minute

segundo

second

¿Hablas español?

Do you speak Spanish?

¿Cómo te llamas?

What is your name?

¿Qué día es hoy?

What day is today?

Hoy es lunes.

Today is Monday.

¿Cómo estás?

How are you?

Estoy bien.

I am fine.

¡Mucho gusto!

Pleased to meet you!

¡Buenos días!

Good morning!

¡Buenas tardes!

Good afternoon!

¡Buenas noches!

Good night!

¡Hasta luego!

See you later!